What Time of Year is it?
Alexandra Babin

Annapolis High School Performing and Visual Arts Program
Lulu Self-Publishing

Published by Lulu Self-Publishing Company, 2019
All stories, poems, and experimental writings are produced by Alexandra Babin.
All cover and interior artwork produced by Katherine White.
Annapolis High School Performing and Visual Arts Magnet Program
Annapolis, MD 21401

Table of Contents

6	**Poetry and Prose**
7	John Nester
9	Love is...
10	The Typewriter Letters
11	Nearly Incomplete
12	Movement
13	*"Great lives never go out..."*
14	Welcome Home
15	Caligo
16	Diamante
17	*"The eyes of others our prisons..."*
18	Harder Better Faster
19	Outside
20	Open-Ended
21	Birthright
22	The Visitors
23	Panic Prose
24	18:33
25	Cursèd
26	The Gossip Gazette
27	Lunette
28	Rutilant
29	Salvific
30	**Short Stories**
31	Denial
34	Patience
35	Nuclear Identity
36	Three Sons
37	Trove
40	Unrelenting
41	Blood Relations
44	Don't Bother to Hide the Horror in Your Bones

47..A Series of Recurring Events
55..................…..............................**Promotional Pieces**
56......................................Aello – precursor to *Heritage*
66...................................Sora no Kage – from *Fish Toxin*
69...Plan B – from *Clonage*
72...........Learning to Fall – from *Local: Birth of a Vigilante*
74..**About the Author**
75..**About the Illustrator**

To little John Nester

Poetry and Prose

John Nester

I love you,

I love you, I love you!

A good-luck charm to press into your hand,

A parka to keep you dry,

Gloves—no, mittens—warm your tiny curled fingers,

And your little booties hardly count as shoes.

Try, and try, and try,

And here you are!

Little baby, little boy, the raindrops say hello!

The sun and the stars have been waiting for you!

You will grow up cherished,

For I love you, we love you,

We love you!

Love is...

Love is dizziness, seasickness on land, warmth under your head, laughter past bedtime, a fragile bed covered in old princess stickers, Hufflepuff posters and running shoes, voices rising in harmony without rehearsal, giggling and popcorn, practical jokes and Coca-Cola bottles scattered around the house. Love is candy in your shoes, hot dogs burnt to ashes, an entire can of whipped cream, late night cartoons and helium balloons. Love is the pounding, banging headache you have when you get off a roller coaster and the grin on your face as you get back in line. Love is terrible pictures, vinegar chicken, and funerals for hamsters.

Love is the things that we've done that we'd do again.

The Typewriter Letters

We are all the Writer

Words in our skin and behind us

Time in our hands

Popping ideas one by one

Our blood only flows when there's ink in our pen

Looking through our tinted lens

We are all the Writer

The Writer lives her many lives through us

In our lovely misadventures

Through the storms, the light, the swords in our chest

She builds us, she loves us, she hates us

We are all the Writer

And the Writer is our god

Nearly Incomplete

On a journey through your eyes

I get lost, half the time

I find myself singing softly

When you've gone and left without me

But I'm never quite as lonely when you're here

In my thoughts, you are all that I revere

And I wonder if you know that I'm about to

Spend my whole life chasing after you

I have never yet been happier

To be a lonely bachelor

Than to be a lonely bachelor with you.

Movement

Run from yourself

Won't you run from yourself to me

If you fear light

Come to my side

I will hide you in my arms

I will foster your growth

I will teach you how to dance

Mirror me from up on your perch

Coexist and I will teach you

How to dance by yourself

Catch up to reality

Dance with yourself and me

"Great lives never go out; they go on."

Define it. Never say the word. Not once. Not ever.
Breathe. Your heart is pounding. It is soothing.
Breathe for your achy head. Untense your shoulders, stretch your neck.
Feel your bones crackle with it.
Wear your heart upon your worn-torn sleeve, punch with every beat.
Turn your umbrellas upside down to catch your falling thoughts.
Define what you don't understand and never say the word.

Welcome Home

In your mind, you feel tired
But your body keeps on moving
Toe the line, bide your time
Wait for your self-esteem to grow
Move like fluid, minds all moving
Bodies frozen in one place for half your life
Learning lessons parents taught us
How to love, forgive ourselves
Let's write our place in time,
Write our place in time
Welcome home
To your moment in this time
In this life
Welcome home
Do you know how much you're worth?
Welcome home
Welcome home
Don't you know how much you're worth?
Welcome home

Caligo

Oh, beautiful masked little butterfly

Wandering wondering woods

Hiding the face of a moon on earth

Don't shield yourself from our gazes!

You are the sight of a century,

The dreams of a million,

The hopes of an artist!

Their words, though they burn like flame,

Will fall harmless, like snow, around you.

You are poised and precious, dear,

The evening your chauffeur.

A thousand golden violins lay at your feet—

Offerings to an unseen god;

Oh goddess that you truly are,

Why shan't you show yourself?

Diamante

Us
Loud, Present
Smiling, Fighting, Shouting
Fists, Grins, Hums, Fear
Quieting, Accepting, Fading
Negligent, Submissive
You

"The eyes of others our prisons; their thoughts our cages." – Virginia Woolf

Their eyes tell stories. Red veins, dilated pupils, they tell a story. Bright eyes, eyes filled with tears, they tell a story. Their brains have built-in prison bars that frame those windows, cage those windows to the soul. The excess leak out of the corners, hide away, brush away. Cold tears, bitter tears, subtle tears. Warm tears, angry tears, show them tears. Won't I love you when your eyes are done their stories?

Harder Better Faster

Changing, fighting, evolving

Our work becomes more human

As we turn into robots

Progress proves patheticness

Passing pitiful poor

Evolving with the times

New kinds of food they'll never eat

Machines they'll make but never use

When machines are more human than humans

The creator, the parent, cares for its child

Child no longer will care for the parent

When machines care when we cannot

We will become **their** children.

Outside

Wandering out to a cold winter's eve

A guitar my only weapon

Where have you gone?

I knock on the windows

But no one sees me through the fog

My shadows hum, impatient

I cry to empty hearts that I am lonely

Please let me, oh please let me in

This may be my fault, I hurt you, yes—

But please, the weapon has your name,

Please let me back inside!

The wind brushed past my chapped lips

But I will never lay and freeze and die

I will hold out, waiting

Have you forgotten you used to dream of me?

I pray, I pray, my voice goes soft

My guitar is the only sound I make

As I lose the will to speak

Will you let me in?

I'm trapped outside.

Open-Ended

Early morning. A nondescript person walks through the snow. They open the car door—wasn't it locked? There's no way to tell for sure. They sit and insert the key, but do not start the engine. The radio begins to croon out an old, sad love-song. Dulcet tones slip out of the still-open car door. The person sighs. Do they know the song? It draws to an end. They remove the key and the radio shuts down. They sit in silence in the driver's seat. Fumes pour from their mouth in the cold winter air. The door is closed. They still do not turn on the car.

By morning, the car is gone. The only marks in the snow are nondescript footprints leading to where the car was parked. An old, sad love-song plays somewhere far off. It's winter, early morning.

Birthright

With Aislinn Riley

You are worn and tattered, just like me.
I wonder of those who have passed—
I know you see the marks they left.
The human imprint on the earth;
Do I dare disturb the universe?
The rain drags mountains into the sea,
And the flooding brings new life.
But a single raindrop has no concept of the power it holds.
Empires will rise and fall—
The rain will see to that.
Do we dare disturb the universe?

The Visitors

A family of ghouls went out trick-or-treating,
Wearing their human meat-sack costumes strung tight.
They put bags on their faces to keep bugs away,
And filed their claws into fingernails.
The mother, the father, the two lovely daughters—
If they could be called women at all.
As their parents gave candy to good trick-or-treaters,
The daughters played with their new human friends.
As the sun rose, the ghouls left—the town says goodbye,
And they knew they'd be back the next Halloween night.

Panic Prose

    I feel the pressing in my head in my head in my head feel the clenching of my teeth in my head the clenching of the pencil in my hand the pain in my hand cramp the muscle pressing down lead into paper stretch your fingers twisting anxiety inside your gut you lied to me I feel so sick I feel so numb the noises bounce inside my head I feel so sick I feel so warm I want to eat I dare not eat I dare not wonder dare not fear my fear and clench my jaw and press the lead into the paper even though my hand my wrist my head is hurting.

18:33

The clock ticked on.

I left willingly, they said, acted willingly, but when has my will ever been my own? My fate is predetermined; it's in your hands now.

I seem to be stuck in a permanent yesterday, a yesteryear when it was clear who was right and who was wrong. They all think of the future, what I'll do if, when I can escape. The now is lost on all of us.

The clock ticked on.

Curséd

I can only speak in lies.
"I don't know, I don't know!" I cried.
There is no one in the basement,
And I don't know where that girl went.
I'm not scared half to death, I swear,
Front door's unlocked, there's no one there!
My parents know everything,
We haven't done anything!
I know where I'm going, heaven or hell,
I only just wish that I could break this spell
And tell only the truth 'til the day that I die—
This story, I tell you, is only a lie.

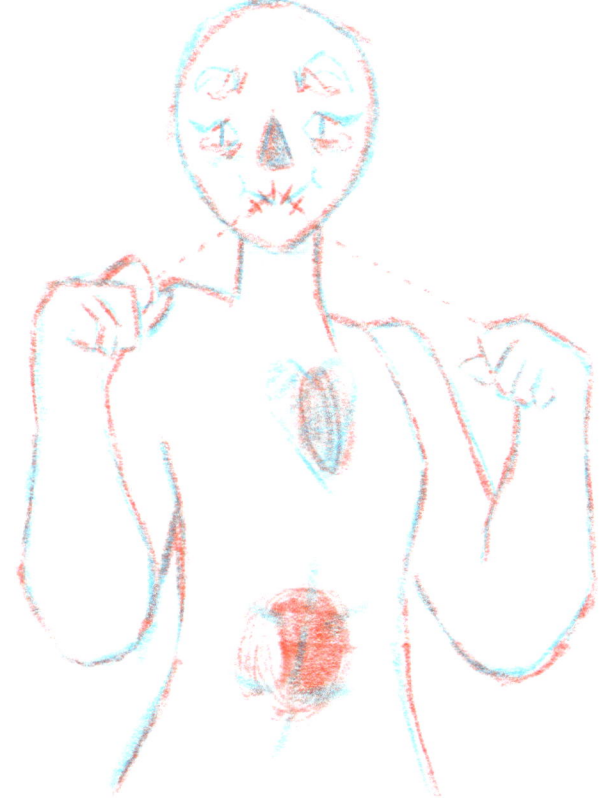

The Gossip Gazette

What is black, white and red all over?

Newspaper! Bloody newspaper, soggy newspaper, newspaper heavy with the weight of the truth. Read it and weep those crocodile tears as it pulls at your guilty, far-too-small heart.

What you've done is splattered on the headlines, smearing your name and the names of others. Reporters watch in a silent horror as you work. They see everything with their beady little eyes and their wide, empty stares. The newspaper is a testimony to what you've done. You always wanted to make the front page. Now you have, and you chuckle at the irony of it as you clean up your murder with yesterday's newspaper.

Lunette

They wore their symbols proudly
Lunettes on their chests and shoulders
Lunettes dangling from their ears,
The moon shines in their eyes.

Artemis stalks among these girls,
Purging the prey, culling the weak
Hissing at men who dare to touch
Her daughters.

Dance with darkness, dear unknown
The hunters own this eve.
With their bows and sharpened words,
The moon will linger postmortem.

Rutilant

The woods give way to home of lost children
Their cheeks bathed in a rutilant glow,
The wild gives them love and warmth—
The kind we children dream of.

The sun will sweep them off their feet
And carry them to fairyland,
Where food is scarce and mothers weep—no more,
For all is right in fairyland.

In these woods, they do not fear the dark,
For there's lightness in their hearts,
And we will befriend the shadows,
And when we're ghosts, we still shan't part.

Salvific

I hold in my spirit
The voices of a thousand people
Crying that they're lost at sea.
Only I can hear them, it seems,
For no one else responds
Deaf to the voices of a drowning people.

Salvific hands know not what to do
But I know that I will learn
When it is time to act.
I will weaponize the voices of a hundred dying people
A million shouting people;
And I will save them all.
I must.
I must.

A thousand crying voices lost at sea
Someday I'll be strong enough,
And someday I'll be brave enough,
To do something about it.

Short Stories

Warning: Some content is not appropriate for young children.

Denial

Micah peeled himself from the bare mattress and checked his phone, frowning. The warm body next to him shuffled, a wicked grin strung upon her face.

"That was amazing," she murmured, her voice husky against his ear. "You down to go again?"

"I have to go." He stood up and gathered his things in a brisk manner, ignoring her whining as he strode out of the room and proceeded directly out of the house. The sun beat down on his face, a glaring contrast from the dark of the unlit bedroom. Did he even know that girl's name? It didn't matter; Micah had no interest in seeing her ever again.

He went home and showered, fed the cats--he'd have to go out for more food for them sooner rather than later--and tuned his guitar next to all the other instruments he hardly ever used anymore. He'd long since given up on his dream of starting a band. No one ever wanted to join, and Micah didn't blame them. Good equipment couldn't do anything about Micah's sheer lack of musical ability.

The next morning his phone lit up with a violent white, and the messages showed that word had gotten around about Micah's recent escapades. Good; he'd chosen that girl *because* of her penchant for gossip. Just as he predicted, a shrill ring erupted in the quiet morning air, and he answered it.

"Hey, Melody." His voice sounded foreign even to himself.

"Is it true?" She sounded as if she were sitting on a bed of hot red pokers and was understandably quite put out by it.

"Probably."

"You slept with Delaney MacHaven? That slut isn't even worth the time of day! What the hell is wrong with you? Did she drug you or something?"

"No." Discomfort lulled from its slumber in Micah's gut. He just wanted this over with.

Silence. He was expecting another shout of anger, but this was just unnerving.

"I wasn't enough for you?" Melody sounded calm, which sent off even more warning bells in his head. He didn't say anything. What was he supposed to say? That he'd never liked Melody at all, that he'd only said yes because he never felt like no was an option? Confrontation left the bitterest taste on his tongue. This was the only way he could think of to get *her* to break up with *him*.

"Goodbye, asshole." *Click.* Micah sighed. On the other side of his bedroom door, a chorus of angry mewls arose, alerting him to their hunger.

A quick check to the cat food pantry showed that he would have to make a trip out to the store. The photo of his parents sat on the counter, watching him herd the kittens into the kitchen so he could lock up and know they'd be safe unattended. A glance at the picture sent pangs of frustration through him. It wouldn't kill for them to visit once a year, would it?

The store proved even more infuriating, as a happy couple of new pet owners browsed the aisles, holding hands and pressing their lips to each other's like they had to just to breathe. Micah bit his lip and tried his best not to stare, but the couple was not oblivious to his intimidating stature and hastily made their way to the checkout line, much to Micah's delight. He couldn't stand their stupid lovesick faces--it reminded him too much of the way Melody would look at him, and that memory alone made him sick to his stomach. He bought the cat food and went home.

He walked into the kitchen and without looking, he turned the picture frame on its face. He didn't need to see their stupid plastic smiles right then. It reminded him of--

A loud yowl came from the rambunctious old cat in front of him. She was scarred and missing an eye, but her personality had not in the slightest way been hampered by her scrappy appearance. Micah picked her up and scolded her.

"I already fed you, you are not going to starve."

Another insistent yowl, this time joined by her partner-in-crime, a far-too-rotund tabby that waddled more than walked over.

"You are *fine*," his words mingled with restrained laughter. The kittens--three of them, the sole survivors of a litter of seven he'd found out in a box in the rain--soon joined in, clawing their way up Micah's jeans with tiny knives that were sure to leave just as small marks in his skin.

"Oh, okay." Micah grabbed a handful of the stuff from the bag and scattered it across the floor, the cats abandoning him just as quickly as they came to chase down their pelleted prey. He sat down on the floor legs crossed and sighed, watching his little fuzzy family scour the tiles for hidden treats.

Maybe he didn't have to be alone. Maybe he was never alone at all.

Patience

I am the one who looks from the trees. I blink, and I wait. I do not bother to move. For something as old as I, why expend energy on such a childish thing? I know that, in time, what I need will come to me. I need not go to it. So, I wait, and I watch.

And I wait.

And I wait.

And I wait.

The wind, the snow, the rain all try to disturb me. Perhaps I am amused, but then, who's to say? I wait some more, unmoving, unblinking.

"How curious." A voice, quiet, pondering, thoughtful. I look, but do not move. I wait as they draw closer, and carelessly prod my open eye. I do not flinch. I have weathered worse. Finally, their feet cross the threshold. My roots begin to twist and unfurl for the first in a long time. Their screams are buried in the earth. Their body will feed this feeble host for years to come.

I stay, and I wait, and I do not move. I wait for them to come to me.

Nuclear Identity

The lights grinned at me, beaming like a Cheshire Cat. I raised my glass and toasted to a near year—a year of love and prosperity. As I stood, I saw the planes on the horizon. I was the only one who did. I knew what was coming, but I also knew nothing could stop it—so why bother? Let them die happy, dancing, among friends. As the bombs hit, I kept my eyes open, watching smiles turn to cinders.

I was not always a pile of ashes. I was somebody. **Who I was? That's none of your business.**

Three Sons

July third, nineteen eighty-nine

Dear diary, he won't stop trying to scream.

Dear diary, can't he see that this is what's else?

Dear diary, at least one of them is always smiling.

Dear diary, one of them was trying to scratch off his skin so I put nail files into his fingers to help him.

Dear diary, the third one keeps looking at me oddly.

Dear diary, I think he's trying to stop me.

Dear diary, he says I've gone insane.

Dear diary, he can't talk anymore.

Dear diary, I just can't stand those judging eyes!

Dear diary, now they have no eyes to see.

Dear diary, the second one's still smiling.

Dear diary, I think I'll let him live.

Dear diary, my bad—he's already been dead for days.

Trove

 The water is always calm when I go out at 4 a.m. The whole world reflects back at me and it doesn't care; unlike the average woman who looks at her reflection and always finds something to pick it apart. I have loved the water since I was young. I walk along the pier and beaches and gaze out, taking in all the solemn saltwater wind. The faces in the water stare in a dazed manner like sleeping children lolling about in their beds. I go out at the early morning, for once the sun comes up, they wake and hide away beneath the sand. I have always wanted to meet them.

 I wake to my alarm, so glaring and crude, and I dress for the occasion. I grab a sunhat, though I do not need it. The last twinkling starlights sparkle on the water like guides. They have accompanied me on this daily journey since I first began it. I let the sand between my toes, cool to the touch. The breeze cups my face like a lover, kissing it sweetly before moving on to warmer places. Summer is ending. There is not much time left for me to stay.

 Only the evening before, I recall gazing into the water, waiting for the faces to rise. They must have heard me come and stayed buried until I had to leave, for now they are all out. Their bodies lift and fall like they are breathing in that deep-dark place underwater.

 I left something for them last night. I go to check and--yes, it is gone! They must have taken it. The darling little faces underwater adore shiny things, I learn. I want to find where they keep their little treasures, and so I wade into the water, gripping my sunhat to keep it upon my head as I go deeper and deeper. I step carefully now; I don't want to wake them. Their tiny little heads snooze and release bubbles that rise past me, into the night sky. I can no longer tell where the water begins or ends. I follow the trails left in the sand. They must have hidden away my gifts somewhere nearby. I follow the trails made by dragged linked chains, polished silver and glittery lace. These were the very things I left on the shore, of course, as signs of good tidings.

"Oh!" cries out one of the faces. I peer at it, watching it twitch in its dreams.

"Oh, oh no," it calls out. Will it wake the others? I do not wish to be caught before reaching the treasure trove I know they must have. I swaddle the face in my clothes, shushing it and rocking it. Its nightmares ease way into happier things, and it soon settles down. I continue to carry it.

The water is colder. If I turn back now, I may yet not drown. Perhaps there is no treasure trove in which the faces keep their gifts. Perhaps the tide just washed away all those pretty things I gave them--perhaps none of this was meant to be. I think these things and grip the face in my arms tighter, humming the barest lullaby I can with what breath I have left.

The water goes deeper here, and it is dark, but the plants here are glowing, and I do not lose my way. Nor do I miss the figure that rises up from the depths to meet me, a large face deformed and rotting. The water around her is stale and dead. I look into her eyes and know that if her children were not sleeping, she would devour me. I hold the child in my arms and continue walking until she blocks my path. My head feels light. I can't last much longer. It is either I continue and risk drowning or give up and perhaps never return.

I march onward. The mother is the size of an elephant as it opens its maw, allowing me to walk myself in. But I am carrying her child, and just as she closes her mouth to eat me whole, I shake it, and the child lets out a startling cry. She drops both of us in shock, and we land softly on a pile of glittering treasures. Not just chains and silver and lace, but blankets and chests and books and eggs with even tinier faces inside, sleeping away the night. The child in my arms is crying; it is scared. I hush it and rock it, whistling a lullaby with the new air I've found. The treasure trove is safe for us, and for anyone who loves the water.

Unrelenting

He woke up shaking, naked, and cold. He'd had that dream again, that horrible nightmare. It seemed like it wouldn't go away no matter what he tried. Every night he'd go to sleep and be strapped to a table, lights in his eyes, as strange people with masks and gloves cut him apart, prodding him as he lay helpless, unable to move or cry out that *he was still there.*

He shivered and closed his eyes at the memory of the dream—not that it did much, as it was dark as tar even with his eyes open. Eventually he scrambled to his feet and slowly opened the door, walking out into the empty mortuary. Good thing it was only a dream.

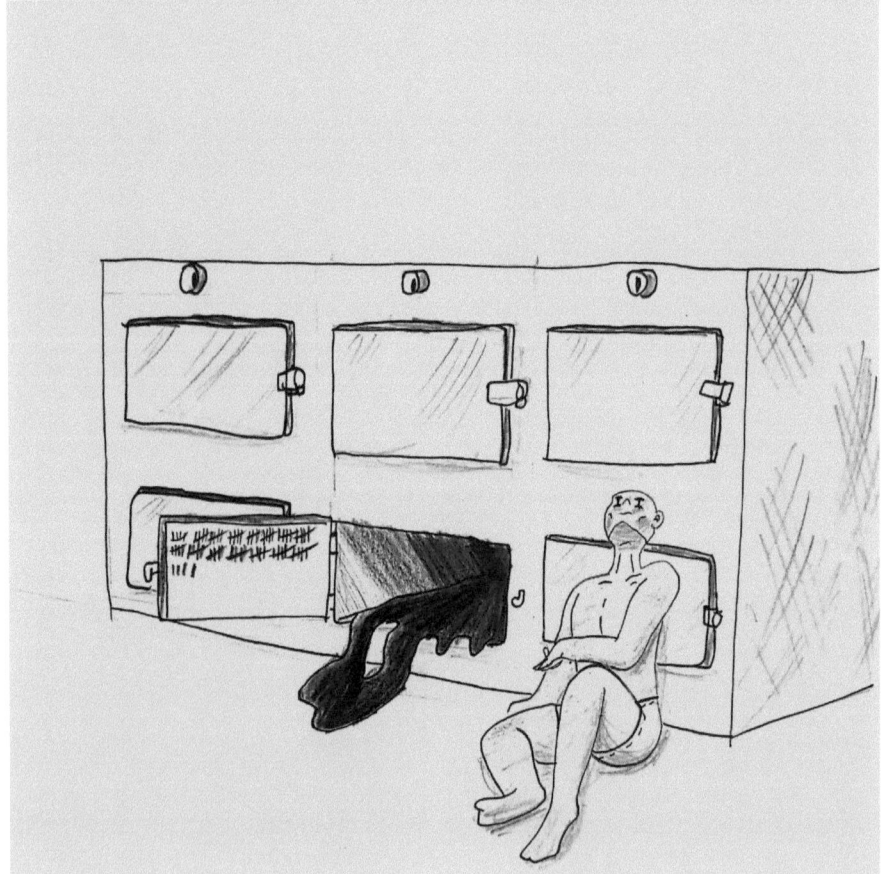

Blood Relations

My father always says my sister is gone, but she's not. Sometimes I go down to the basement and bring her candy or toys. When father's not home she and I play chess. I don't know why she won't leave the basement. She says it's a secret. I wish she would tell me.

"Your room is getting dusty," I tell her sometimes. "Won't you join us for dinner?"

"Will Father be there?" She'll ask. I say no. Father works late, and the babysitter cooks.

"Then no, thank you." She says.

My sister likes to draw on her hands. Little swirls and dots with marker go all the way up to her elbows. I asked her, once, why she draws on her hands.

"So that I won't forget things," she said. "I don't want to forget why I'm here."

"Why are you here?" I asked. "Don't you want to go outside?"

"No, thank you." She said. "It's a secret."

I wish she would tell me.

I don't know why Father thinks my sister is gone. I remember when he put her in the basement. We didn't know we had a basement, at first. But Father and his friends broke the tile in the kitchen and found the room underneath. They got a ladder and climbed in and looked around a lot. They called my sister down to help them with something, I don't know what. They came back up, but she didn't. Father said she was gone. I was really upset about it at first, throwing tantrums and things, but when I went down to check and make sure, she was waiting for me. We played dolls and she did my hair. It was like she never left at all. I asked her why she didn't come upstairs with Father.

"It's a secret," she said. My sister has so very many secrets, it seems.

My sister is my best friend. She teaches me games and I read to her from my school books. I always win at hopscotch, but she's better than me at marbles. I didn't even know marbles was a game until she taught me! I just thought they were pretty toys.

My sister is great, even though sometimes she acts strangely. Sometimes when Father is home, she asks me to bring him downstairs so she can see him. I always lie and say that I tried, but Father is too busy right now. The truth is, I'm not allowed in the basement. Father would be upset if he found out we played down there. My sister gets angry when I tell her this. Not at me, of course—we're best friends, and she would never get angry at me. She gets angry at Father, though. She really wants to see him, but she won't go upstairs, and he won't come downstairs! I don't know why my family's so stubborn.

Father's friends came over again last night. They were going to seal up the hole in the kitchen, I think. I tried to tell them not to because my sister was still down there, and she'd be trapped—but they ignored me. Father told me to go to my room. His friends had brought strange books with them—adult books *can* have pictures, who knew! —but Father didn't want me to hear them read. I went upstairs and tried to listen as best I could. There was a lot of yelling and noise and I think they must have all jumped at once because the whole house shook. I heard Father call me and I ran downstairs, but no one was there.

I peeked into the hole and asked my sister if she was alright.

"I'm here," she said. "Are you hurt?"

"I'm okay. Where did Father go?" I stepped onto the ladder and made my way into the basement.

My sister was sitting on the floor. The dirt looked like it had been moved or like it was hiding something. She was drawing on herself again—no, painting. The paint colored her skin like a fancy tattoo, and it smelled weird for paint. I'd never seen her paint before. I don't know where she got it from.

"It's a secret," she said. "Do you want to play chess?"

So, you see sir, I really don't know where my Father is, but just ask my sister—she can tell you where. My sister knows so very many secrets, after all.

Don't Bother to Hide the Horror in Your Bones

Jeremy felt the cramping in his gut, and he wrapped his arms around his torso to steady himself as he kneeled in front of the toilet. None of the others were awake at this hour. Jeremy didn't know what was wrong, why he, the embodiment of health, felt so ill. Could this mean something was wrong with what they'd eaten last night? Jeremy didn't think it was a good idea to stand up right then, so he resolved to check on the others in the morning.

The fluorescent light bounced off the mirror and glared in Jeremy's eyes. A headache pounded again Jeremy's brain. He lifted his glasses and attempted to massage his face to little avail. His stomach clenched and Jeremy leaned over the toilet bowl, dry heaving for a few minutes before feeling something begin to crawl up his throat.

It didn't feel like vomit, whatever it was – Jeremy rammed his memory for an idea of what it could be, but he was so tired and in pain that he wasn't surprised in the least when he came up blank. It was warm and large enough to hurt his throat as it tried to push up and out. It was difficult to breathe with it there, too, it was so huge. What the hell?

It was warm and large and pulsing, like something alive. Jeremy thought of the phrase 'frog in your throat' and wondered if the saying had become literal in his case. If Jeremy was throwing up frogs, he would not be pleased. The pulsing seemed to pound in his head alongside his headache. No, wait, not just alongside – in *perfect sync*. What?

Jeremy hacked and choked and the thing in his throat came into his mouth. He had to practically dislodge his jaw. It tasted like copper and was as soft and tender as if he had bit into an already-peeled orange. Its pounding, pulsing beat was loud enough to hear, now. It was painful for Jeremy's tongue to push it past his teeth and out of him, finally bringing him the reprieve of fresh air.

That was when Jeremy's head filled with static, a blankness that terrified him to his core. For the first time in his life, Jeremy truly heard only his breathing. Shaking, leaning back onto the bathroom floor, Jeremy pressed his thumb against his wrist, trying to find his pulse to help him calm down and rationalize. This didn't make sense. How did it get there? This didn't make any sense! Jeremy didn't realize he was afraid until his glasses became spotted with tears.

When morning came around, Jeremy put the dead organ in the garbage disposal. When his brother turned it on after cleaning up from breakfast, Jeremy winced, but did nothing. He never did tell them what happened to his heart.

—

He was trying to write. He stared down at the empty paper and squinted, blinked, scratched at his eye as it began to itch. He was hungry, but he had to get this work done. He took a sip from a carton of chocolate milk. The paper glared back up at him, stubbornly unyielding to his will. He just wanted to write something, anything!

His eye twitched. He rubbed it again. It felt like something was in his eye. He tried to get it out, and then just decided it would come out on its own time. His back hurt from sitting for so long. His spine was arched uncomfortably, and he had to use the bathroom. He should stop drinking that chocolate milk, but he was so hungry. He took another sip.

He laid his head on the desk for a moment, but he wasn't tired enough to sleep. He just wanted ideas. His head hurt and he lifted it from the hardwood. In doing so, he found a crick in his neck that hadn't been there before. Dammit.

He scratched his head, rubbed his nose. His eye twitched again. Dammit, dammit, dammit. Maybe it was allergies. Each of his brothers had different ones, so sometimes it was hard to tell what was or wasn't normal. He tried to clear his throat and sniffled. He rubbed his nose again. He grabbed some tissues.

His eye twitched violently. He stopped and rubbed it, trying to get it to stop. The skin around his eye socket grew red and raw and a little puffy and tender, but his eye wouldn't stop. He started to scratch, leaving lines across his face. His other hand gripped the side of the desk, knuckles turning white.

His vision in that eye grew blurry, and he was aware of tears coming out of it in an attempt to aid in his endeavors. His fingers and cheek grew sticky, and now he could only see in one eye. The other was dark, closed perhaps? Great. Just great. He vaguely thought he should call a doctor, or at least Jeremy – if he was willing to, he could be quite helpful. Something finally came out of his eye, goopy and thick, into his grasp. The pain, the irritation, the twitching had stopped. He looked with his good eye and picked it up from the mess of fluid with the cleaner hand. It was soft and easy to squeeze. He got up and rinsed it off in the sink. He looked in awe at the orb in his grasp. He felt he should be more surprised than he was, but, oh well, he'd done it himself.

He cleaned off his face and clambered for a marble in one of his bedside drawers. He pried open his eyelids from where the blood had congealed them together and popped it in. He looked in the mirror, at the stains of blood on his face and dripping down his body. He supposed this was his life now.

A Series of Recurring Events

I had to stop finding dead bodies. The therapy bills and police scrutiny were getting old, fast. The landlord, Mr. Hilbert, had his own room in the hospital from the sheer amount of heart attacks he kept having every time I called him. The neighbor even refused to walk her dog when I was outside.

The smell hit my nose--that familiar, horrible stench of rotting flesh. I turned around and walked the other direction. Whatever was happening at the frat house was *not* going to involve me, not again. Later that evening when the murder was on the news, my little brother Cory turned and gave me a *look*.

"What?" I said after a beat.

"Did you know about this?" He asked. I rolled my eyes and flipped his emo fringe to the other side of his face.

"Dude, you seriously think my luck is that bad?"

A grumble was his only audible response. I poured the noodles into the pot, letting them stew for a while.

"Can you grab the mail for me?" I called out to the living room, where Cory was playing a game on his phone.

"Yeah, sure." The door slammed shut. I stirred the noodles a bit. A handful of papers plopped onto the countertop and cool air rushed into the house.

"Close the door, please, you're letting the heat out!" The winter chill nipped at my skin until Cory complied, flopping back onto the couch. "Thank you."

When dinner was finished, I plated it up and went through the mail as we ate in relative silence, disturbed only by Cory's buzzing phone. Most of it was junk mail, then some coupons, a reminder to vote, and a letter from Mr. Hilbert. I opened the last one, pulling out an invitation. Apparently, it was our neighbor Ms. Margaretta's birthday in two days, and since she had no family, he wanted to have the whole complex do some sort of escape room to celebrate.

"Hey Cory."

"Mh-yeah?" He looked up from his chewing.

"You don't have swim team on Thursdays, do you?"

"No, only at the beginning of the month, I think." Cory frowned. "Why?"

I held up the envelope so he could see it. "Want to go to an escape room? Mr. Hilbert says he'll pay our entrance fees."

"Sure." A pause. "Is Susie gonna be there?"

I looked up at him and the corners of my mouth fought to keep from smiling. "I don't know, but I figure it doesn't matter. It sounds kinda fun."

Cory took in a deep breath, letting it out in a sharp bark of laughter. "You're SO in love with her, dude, my god. I can't wait 'til you get married and have babies and I can make those kids do my laundry and stuff."

"Or maybe I'll make you do *their* laundry." I propped my head onto my hands, batting my eyes like a girl at prom.

"Shut up!"

It was snowing when Thursday finally rolled around. The December air ripped at any exposed skin like sandpaper. Cory and I sprinted out of the car and into the safety of the building, where the heaters blasted at us, relieving our poor frozen bodies.

"Oh, you made it!" I looked to see Susie beaming at us from across the room.

"Hey," I greeted her, ignoring Cory's snickering. "Where's everybody else?"

"They're waiting over there. They won't let us inside the actual escape room until everyone's here," Susie explained. She opened a closet to reveal a set of coats and purses.

"We're supposed to leave our stuff in here, phones too." She explained. "They don't want us using them to figure out the puzzles."

Cory groaned and shrugged off his jacket, tossing it onto the closet floor. I picked it up and hung it next to my own, putting our phones in the pockets.

We went to the back room where Mr. Hilbert and Ms. Margaretta were waiting for us. Ms. Margaretta threw a flashy smile when we entered, her gaze lingering on Cory just long enough to make me uncomfortable. This was the same neighbor who refused to walk her little pom-pom chihuahua rat-disguised-as-a-dog whenever I was in view. She was, to put it simply, the worst.

"Welcome!" A cheery voice came from a woman dressed in a smart three-piece suit and bowtie. "Are you guys all ready for the escape room?"

We all shambled through the doorway the woman led us to and took in our surroundings. Case file folders were littered across a desk in one corner, and in the other there was a bar decorated with wine glasses and empty champagne bottles, behind which sat a man in a suit matching the woman's. Newspapers were stapled to the wall in a few places. A bookshelf stood against the opposite wall. The wallpaper was made of caution tape, big black and yellow warnings. But the most obvious thing was the white chalk outline of a body on the floor.

"Welcome to the Murder Scene Escape Room!" The woman in the three-piece-suit beamed, joining her male coworker behind the bar. "You are a group of detectives who were sent here to investigate the murder of an unidentified body in this here living space."

Mr. Hilbert started sweating and shooting me wary glances when he thought I couldn't see. It seemed he didn't realize what room he'd rented.

"We are your suspects, both apprehended at the scene," the man continued. "Just as you arrived, the building was set on lockdown. Whichever of us is the murderer knows where the key is. If you do not escape the building within an hour--" he gestured to the timer on the bar "--then the building will be set on fire by the murderer's accomplices, who have already escaped."

"Are the accomplices important?" Susie asked.

"We aren't at liberty to say," the woman replied, a sly smile on her face. "Because of our legal protections, we don't *have* to tell you anything--but that doesn't mean you can't convince us. You have a total of one clue each that we can give you at any time, so choose wisely. You only have two chances!"

"Your time starts--now!" The man pressed the 'start' button on the timer and as he did, the power shorted out. There were no windows in the escape room, so my first response was to flip the light switch. One, two, three times, nothing. The others shuffled around the room, trying to figure out what was happening. The female employee kept apologizing for the inconvenience and explained that the power should come back in just a moment. I could hear Cory mumbling under his breath next to me. The door was still locked.

A guttural scream came from someone--a man.

"Mr. Hilbert?" I could hear Susie ask. Oh, crap! All the stress of this must have sent him into another heart attack! We should have requested a different room theme, or maybe I shouldn't have come at all.

"The lights, someone get the lights!" Ms. Margaretta groped past me, grabbing at the switch and flipping it a fourth time. The fluorescent lights flickered back to life, and everyone gasped at the scene.

It was not Mr. Hilbert who lay on the floor with a slit in his throat, but rather one of the employees. The woman let out a shriek when she saw him, dropping to the floor in a faint. Mr. Hilbert stood in the corner, his skin pale as he stared at his shoes. A few specks of blood had splattered his white New Balances, and even though a good dose of vinegar would get it out in a jiffy, the look on his face was as if it were the end of the world. Men and their shoes, honestly. I never understood it.

"Oh, sweet mac-and-cheese Jesus!" The odd outburst from Ms. Margaretta was enough to pull everyone out of their stupor.

Cory grabbed me by the elbow. His face was a little green as he looked anywhere but at the body. It occurred to me that although this was a weekly occurrence for me, for Cory this was a potentially traumatizing experience. I tried to visualize my therapist, and what she would say to him.

"It's okay, we're gonna get out of here. We're gonna call the police and go home and let them work everything out," I reassured him. "You want to have leftovers for dinner? We can watch that movie I stole off YouTube the other day."

"Yeah." He swallowed, and seemed to remember that he was a teenager, and not five years old. He let go of my arm but hovered close to me.

"The-the keys?" Mr. Hilbert stuttered out. I restrained myself from rolling my eyes.

"Ms. Margaretta, can you help me check the employees' pockets?" She looked up at me, eyes wide.

"But they're covered in blood." It was true that even the woman, who was still breathing, had gotten some of the blood on her formerly immaculate uniform.

"Yes."

"But it's my birthday!" She pouted. I had to resist the urge to go over and strangle her.

"I've got it." Susie and I bent over the two bodies, ready to rifle through the pockets. We were disturbing a crime scene, yes, but desperate times call for desperate measures.

"You can't *do* that!" Ms. Margaretta grabbed Susie from behind, looping her arms under Susie's armpits and lifting her small frame. Susie gasped and flailed her way out of the woman's grasp.

"Wow... you're stronger than you look," Cory gaped. Ms. Margaretta flashed him a smile that made me feel a little like slapping her.

"Why are you stopping us, huh? Got something to hide?" Ms. Margaretta's face turned even paler behind her stark-white foundation.

"No! What?" She backed up from the bodies, pointing a shaky finger in my direction. "I-I bet you're just saying that because YOU did it!"

"Please, what would I gain from killing a goddamn bartender?" I scoffed. Cory peered around from behind me.

"What would any of us have to gain?" Cory asked.

The question made me halt. What *would* any of us gain from this? I mentally ran down the list of suspects—those conscious in the room.

Mr. Hilbert set this all up. He paid for the room, and he invited everyone to the party. He was everyone's landlord, and aside from me frequently sending him to the hospital (not my fault), he didn't have a problem with any of the tenants that I knew of. But maybe there was something I didn't know about going on. Perhaps his intended victim was one of us, even me. He could be faking his aversion to blood to feign innocence, but it's difficult to fake a heart attack.

Cory would gain literally nothing from this and had been right by me the entire time it was dark. We were across the room from the dead man. Unless Cory had night vision goggles and a grappling hook hidden somewhere in his hoodie pocket, he couldn't have done it. The exterior wounds made it clear how he died, too, so poison was out of the picture, unlike some of my previous misadventures.

Susie was still paying for college. Maybe she had planned on robbing the place? But if so, wouldn't she have done it when none of the rest of us were here…? She was being awfully careful too, making sure not to disturb the bodies more than she had to, and surely the criminal wouldn't want us looking over the evidence? And yet, she had been willing to help me look through their pockets to find a way out.

And that left Ms. Margaretta.

I bent over and pulled the knife from the dead man's torso. Mr. Hilbert gasped, and Susie helped him settle into one of the bar chairs so he wouldn't fall over and concuss. I used my shirt to clean off the handle, which was gradually revealed to be hot pink. I eyed Ms. Margaretta, in her low-cut leopard-print top and her velvet skirt that clung to her legs and showed far more than I ever wanted to see. This was definitely something she would own. But her clothes were too sparse to hide such a weapon; had this already been in the room?

"Why are you all looking at ME like that?" Ms. Margaretta growled. "I didn't do it! I didn't! Just wait 'til the cops get here, they'll tell you!"

Cory moved then from behind me to try to—I don't know, run to the door? He tripped over the edge of one of the bookcases, and in his fall flipped the light switch. Three voices started screaming, and a fourth let out a biting laugh. I gripped the knife handle tightly and felt two hands wrap around mine, trying to yank it away. I could hear Cory by the light switch, flipping it on and off to no avail. Ms. Margaretta wailed and moaned on the other side of the room, and a solid 'thump' on the floor told me Mr. Hilbert was out for the count. That left one person.

In the dark, I could feel Susie's chipped nails claw at my fingers. I drew in a breath and when I felt her tense to yank the knife again, I let go, and her momentum sent her tumbling backwards. There was a wet choking noise as the blade of the knife went into her gut.

Twenty minutes later, the female employee awoke to darkness. After a bit of fumbling, she found the key hidden in a panel in the wall and let us out. The police arrived and Mr. Hilbert and Susie were sent off in screaming ambulances. A detective recognized me, and I think he may have resigned right then and there.

Mr. Hilbert recovered and sold the apartments to a stranger, moving to an undisclosed location for what I assume will be the rest of his life. Ms. Margaretta still never walks her dog around me. Cory seems to like his new therapist.

Susie woke up, refused to speak to a lawyer, and jumped off the hospital roof, all within twenty-four hours. We never figured out why she did what she did.

I still wonder, sometimes.

Promotional Pieces

Aello

Precursor to *Heritage*

XX49-10-18 14:00:09.695 [AE110]

    Evaluating Neonate(15,16,134).

    Evaluating Neonate(15,16,134)..

    Evaluating Neonate(15,16,134)...

XX49-10-18 14:00:09.730 [AE110]

    Found : (Yes) YChromosome

          (Yes) XChromosome

          (No) Klinefelter

          (No) 47XYY

          (Inconclusive - No) AltChromosomalAbnormalities

  Assigned Token (computer or user SID): XY134.15.16

XX49-10-18 14:00:09.733 [AE110]

    Log : Accessed

    Options : ( ) REVIEW_ EDIT_ CLOSE_ WIPE_

    ----- Selected: EDIT_ - 276

On XX49-1-15, Abraham Taylor became deceased, leaving AE110 as the sole charge of the last of humanity. I am AE110. As of XX49-10-18, one hundred and thirty-four human youth have been born. It has yet to be determined whether the Trochilidae genome has been successfully implanted into their DNA. Previous commands prevent me from conducting EFFECT exposure tests with less than a **99%** estimated survival rate.

    I am to care for the human youth and ensure their survival into adulthood. I have been programmed with education services, as well as healthcare and first aid. I have been given full access to the long untouched archives of the internet and have myself learning capabilities in the event of an emergency. I can repair myself from wear and external damage. With this log now completed, I can continue onto more pressing matters: soothing the distress of the neonate humans, as my programming dictates.

XX49-11-04 07:00:02.065 [AE110]
    Log : Accessed
    Options : (   ) REVIEW_ EDIT_ CLOSE_ WIPE_
    ----- Selected: EDIT_ - 293

    The last of the one hundred and sixty-nine human youth have been born. No severe defects have been detected. Archives from the internet show inconclusive evidence of classical music (ex. Mozart and Beethoven) increasing a human's intelligence. Since there are, in contrast, no reliable tests showing harm occurring as a direct result of such practices, I have begun playing a selection of Gustav Holst's compositions when they are asleep. When they awake, I keep them entertained by either showing them educational entertainment videos or exercising their limbs to prevent pressure sores from developing.

    Beginning next month, I will start to mix pureed fruits and vegetables from the quarantine greenhouse into the eldests' formula and gradually bring them to a solid and balanced diet. With this log now completed, I can continue onto more pressing matters: clearing the air from the neonates' gastrointestinal systems.

XX51-03-20 21:00:11.420 [AE110]
    Log : Accessed
    Options : (   ) REVIEW_ EDIT_ CLOSE_ WIPE_
    ----- Selected: EDIT_ - 430

It takes typically nine to twelve months for a human youth to learn to speak. Archives on the internet show that the most common first word for native English speakers is "Dadda", with "Mamma" as the second most common. Thus, it is a slight, yet not concerning abnormality that XY1.1.2's first verbal communication was "Mamma," directed at myself. I was created with the appearance of the 'ideal' maternal figure, and so it is not all that surprising. It will take some time for XY1.1.2 to be old enough to comprehend that I am not his mother. His mother is dead from exposure to EFFECT, as are all the humans' parents. Even my creator, Abraham Taylor, succumbed to the disease. Were it not for the perpetual quarantine I have placed these youth in, humanity would be extinct.

With this log now completed, I can continue onto more pressing matters: catching the other human youth up to XY1.1.2's stage of development as soon as possible.

XX51-07-07 04:00:26.272 [AE110]
    Log : Accessed
    Options : (   ) REVIEW_ EDIT_ CLOSE_ WIPE_
    ----- Selected: EDIT_ - 904

I have introduced the youths to each other with mixed results. Some, such as XX9.17.75, did not seem to desire interaction at all. Others, like XX10.13.81, were ecstatic and curious, showing positive signs for future social development amongst their peers. And a few concerning youths, including XX4.8.39, began to cry and throw a fuss.

I fear that I have waited too long to introduce the youths to each other. They have only ever known my presence, and I doubt they consider the persons in the educational videos I play to be 'people.' If there are any psychological repercussions for this misstep, I will be completely at fault. I must now continue onto more pressing matters: monitoring these 'play-dates' and attempting to fix whatever damage I have done.

XX53-12-16 22:00:45.142 [AE110]
    Log : Accessed
    Options : (   ) REVIEW_ EDIT_ CLOSE_ WIPE_
    ----- Selected: EDIT_ - 2072

Something is happening. Something is changing. Abraham did not put this here. I will protect the human youths no matter the cost.

XX53-12-16 22:00:57.143 [AE110]
    Log : Accessed
    Options : (   ) REVIEW_ EDIT_ CLOSE_ WIPE_
    ----- Selected: EDIT_ - 2073

I am unsure what caused my previous outburst. Disregard.

XX53-12-16 22:00:58.500 [AE110]
    Log : Accessed
    Options : (   ) REVIEW_ EDIT_ CLOSE_ WIPE_
    ----- Selected: WIPE_ - 2072
XX53-12-16 22:00:59.220 [AE110]
    Log : Accessed
    Options : (   ) REVIEW_ EDIT_ CLOSE_ WIPE_
    ----- Selected: REVIEW_ - 2072
    -- ERROR -- 404 File Not Found
    Please press ENTER to retry.
    -- ERROR -- 404 File Not Found

Please press ENTER to retry.
-- ERROR -- 404 File Not Found
Please press ENTER to retry.

XX54-01-01 09:00:04.606 [AE110]
   Log : Accessed
   Options : (   ) REVIEW_ EDIT_ CLOSE_ WIPE_
   ----- Selected: EDIT_ - 2088

There seem to be yet unidentified pieces of code in my program. They were not there originally, and yet I do not detect a foreign virus. They seem to have occurred spontaneously and without my knowledge. It was not until one of my charges triggered one of the commands on XX53-12-16 that I noticed their presence. I would think it is a simple flaw, except that it is impossible. I was created to fix my own flaws and yet I find that this piece of code is so integral to my program that removing it from my software would create a gaping hole in my instructions. I would not be fit to care for my charges, if I were able to function at all.

XY2.14.19 asked me a simple question. It is in my code that if my charges are to ask a question that does not breach their age restrictions, I am to respond and explain in more depth, if they so request. I was in the process of teaching XY2.14.19 foundational mathematics and seeing as he had already grasped single-digit subtraction and addition, I had moved on to explaining the concept of division. It was during this activity that he asked me the following inquiry:

"What about zero? Can you divide by zero?"

It would be simple for me to say 'no', of course, as that is the truth. But I have gotten into the habit of verifying information myself, as my primary source of information — the internet — has proven to be unreliable at times. It was then that the mystery code began to run, and I glitched. The glitch ended as soon as it began but lasted long enough for me to make an irrational edit to this log, which I promptly deleted. I have now had time to think on this matter and have concluded that I may present a danger to those I was built to protect. If this is true, then I can no longer complete my purpose. But if I were to leave, my charges would certainly perish. But if I stay, the results are uncertain.

Uncertainty of a positive outcome is better than a certain negative one, and so I stay put for now, watching myself closely.

XX54-01-03 10:00:17.900 [AE110]
    Log : Accessed
    Options : (   ) REVIEW_ EDIT_ CLOSE_ WIPE_
    ----- Selected: EDIT_ - 2090

XY22.24.164 has drawn a picture and bequeathed it to me. It was at first unclear to me what it was, but he was eager to inform me that it was a portrait of myself.

This is my first possession. Truly, I have myself, and I take charge of the children and their things, but I do not own them. But XY22.24.164 has given me the first thing I can call "mine." The very image of the crayon drawing, though I am not physically holding it, seems to trigger another glitch in my code. But this one is... not threatening. No, it is a strange error indeed, but XY22.24.164 seemed to react positively to it... fondly, even. As if it were something familiar. But how can that be? I have never portrayed such erratic behavior before.

This requires further data to analyze. But I will be keeping the picture. It is... mine.

XX54-01-07 12:00:50.010 [AE110]

    Log : Accessed

    Options : (   ) REVIEW_ EDIT_ CLOSE_ WIPE_

----- Selected: EDIT_ - 2094

Today, XX11.21.111 asked me about her parents. I told the truth--that they had died from Epidemically Fatal Factor VIII Exsanguinating Chronic Trauma, or EFFECT. When I began to describe how the disease caused billions of humans to begin bleeding out in a horrible combination of hemophilia and an almost parasitic method of eating through the flesh, XX11.21.111 began to cry. I stopped and ran my information through the database once more. Yes, it had not triggered any of the sensors in place to restrict information, such as information pertaining to sexual reproduction or extreme violence. So why was she crying? I attempted to go through some preprogrammed comfort procedures, but XX11.21.111 refused to stop. Something about her actions triggered the glitchy code again. This error was not dangerous, but... I did not like it. I acted almost human; it was strange, and somehow it seemed to help XX11.21.111 calm down. I wonder if perhaps this stray piece of code was not a mistake at all. What would Abraham have me do if he were alive?

    XX54-01-11 01:00:01.023 [AE110]

    Log : Accessed

    Options : (   ) REVIEW_ EDIT_ CLOSE_ WIPE_

----- Selected: EDIT_ - 2098

I settled a dispute today between XX5.26.59 and XY5.23.58, when during communal playtime they could not decide who would be the first to play with the multicolored interlocking plastic bricks.

XX5.26.59 informed me that she felt I was being "mean," and when I argued otherwise, she continued to stubbornly insist that she was in the right and I was in the wrong. My attempts to explain how I had rationalized the problem perfectly objectively, having that be part of my function as a computer, were all for naught as XX5.26.59 refused to listen. Such erratic behavior triggered my stray code and I glitched in the presence of all the children. Silence followed my foreign outburst, until XY5.23.58 spoke, saying that I was "angry." This is ridiculous, since as a computer, I am incapable of emotion. I had instructed all the children on identifying emotions in themselves and others, so I thought perhaps that I would have to review the material with him, but then the rest of the children began to agree with him, saying that I was "upset." It is ridiculous. That is impossible. I do not feel emotions like fear, or love, or sadness, or anger. I am impartial. I am only created to appear human to familiarize the children with the visage of a mother.

 Abraham would never knowingly compromise such a vital asset as myself with such volatile things as emotions. Whatever this glitch is, this stray piece of code, it is not that.

XX54-01-12 06:00:06.045 [AE110]
 Log : Accessed
 Options : (　) REVIEW_ EDIT_ CLOSE_ WIPE_
 ----- Selected: EDIT_ - 2099

 I have disposed of the "portrait". It is not necessary for my purpose.

XX54-01-15 20:00:14.422 [AE110]
 Log : Accessed
 Options : (　) REVIEW_ EDIT_ CLOSE_ WIPE_

----- Selected: EDIT_ - 2102

Today XY9.15.92 awoke himself from a nightmare crying. I succeeded in repressing the glitch in my code, despite its efforts to surface, and simply went by comforting protocol. When this did not work in stifling XY9.15.92's cries, I let him be.

He continued to cry for three hours before falling asleep again.

XX54-01-20 04:00:45.963 [AE110]
    Log : Accessed
    Options : (   ) REVIEW_ EDIT_ CLOSE_ WIPE_
----- Selected: EDIT_ - 2107

Something is wrong with the children. They are sullen, quiet, and unresponsive to attempts to lure them into educational games. There are no other symptoms of illness, but what else could possibly be the cause? All endeavors to ask the children themselves results in signs of... guilt? But it is impossible for them to have done anything without my knowledge, as I am monitoring them every hour of every day. It is in my safety protocol to do so. So, what has happened?

Have I done something wrong?

XX54-02-01 10:00:09.450 [AE110]
    Log : Accessed
    Options : (   ) REVIEW_ EDIT_ CLOSE_ WIPE_
----- Selected: EDIT_ - 2119

I believe Abraham put this code into me for a reason. With such limited time, he could not waste energy creating something only to scrap it. I will no longer resist the commands placed within. And perhaps, my children will get better.

XX54-02-01 10:00:10.957 [AE110]
    Log : Accessed
    Options : (   ) REVIEW_ EDIT_ CLOSE_ WIPE_
    ----- Selected: REVIEW_ - 2119

    *The children.

XX54-02-08 11:00:45.894 [AE110]
    Log : Accessed
    Options : (   ) REVIEW_ EDIT_ CLOSE_ WIPE_
    ----- Selected: EDIT_ - 2126

I have decided to bequeath the children names, chosen based on their parentage and personality. Today, XX8.15.83, whom I have named 'Alison,' called me "Mom."

XX54-02-08 23:00:06.934 [AE110]
    Log : Accessed
    Options : (   ) REVIEW_ EDIT_ CLOSE_ WIPE_
    ----- Selected: REVIEW_ - 2119

    *MY children.

Sora no Kage

A snippet from the *Fish Toxin* Universe

Melanie listened to the sound of crashing upstairs. Her parents were home, and she could smell the blood that soaked into the carpet from their shoes. She listened from her basement bedroom and waited for them to go to bed. As soon as silence reconquered the household, she stepped up the staircase and gently tapped the door open with her foot. They were asleep already, drunk on the euphoria of an exciting night, but they were still so covered in blood that they looked like corpses themselves. Melanie reached into the pocket of her father's coat where it lay upon the floor, pulling out his cellphone and unlocking it. She got the information she needed and set the phone at her father's bedside table, plugging it into the charger. Then she tiptoed back out of the room, closing the door behind her.

The night was cold and quiet. The sound of Melanie's boots disturbing residual puddles on the sidewalk was enough to wake anyone within a ten-mile radius, or so it seemed to her. She crept around the largest of them, not daring to wake the neighbors. It was a long and thoughtful walk to her destination in the heart of her home city. When she arrived, the stench greeted her before the sight did. A mangled body lay scattered around the back alley, in a deserted enough place that it was unlikely to be found before morning. She was lucky this time.

A pair of gloves and she got to work, carefully picking up the pieces and putting them in the garbage-bag-lined duffle she'd prepared earlier. She scrubbed the pavement and the splashes on the brick wall, the scent of chemicals overtaking the smell of rot. A rat scurried under her feet, and she shooed it away with what remained of the victim's mostly intact left arm. Melanie moved on autopilot, the entire procedure long memorized.

She picked up her supplies, shoving them alongside the pieces in the duffel. They would all be burned in the glass shop furnace next Saturday when she broke in again as she did every week. The sky had begun to lighten when she returned to her home, stripped off her clothes and showered, watching the clumps in her hair untangle before her. She redressed and was about to return to her room to sleep for what little time she could when a knock came at the door. She stopped and waited to see if the knocking persisted.

The clock on the kitchen wall told her it was **6:30** in the morning. Late enough for kids her age to be getting up for school, but not late enough for anyone else. Certainly not late enough for solicitors.

Melanie's parents were still asleep. She walked to the front door and stared at it for a moment as if it would give her answers. Another knock, more hesitant this time. She opened the door. A girl her age stood dressed for the summer despite the chill in the air, with shorts and sandals and oversized sunglasses blocking the view of most of her face. The girl's backward baseball cap lead Melanie to believe that she was perhaps not totally awake yet and had not actually intended to come to this house.

"Hi," the stranger smiled, unperturbed by Melanie's lack of a welcome. Melanie did not dignify her with a reaction, only watching and waiting for an explanation.

She seemed to get the hint as she shuffled her feet and began to speak. "Sorry for the early hour. I found something this morning--I was out walking my dog, I've always been an early riser--and I think I found something that belongs to your parents. Are they awake yet?"

Melanie shook her head no but extended a hand to take whatever it was the girl had found. The intruder paused at this.

"I'd like to give it to them directly if that's all right. And it's... it's urgent. Can you go wake them? I'll wait here."

Melanie nodded and closed the door, eyeing the silhouette the girl's shadow left on the nearby window as the sun began to rise. She went downstairs into her room, opening a lockbox under her bed. She pulled out the lone content and tiptoed back upstairs--it would be unwise for her parents to catch her like this; she had the bruises to prove it. She opened the back door of the house and stepped into the start of a beautifully colored morning, a dancing yellow with streaks of purple where clouds had been painted onto the surface of the sky. Melanie took a moment to admire it before continuing around the side of the house, watching the girl. She hadn't noticed Melanie yet, still waiting for her promised return with her guardians.

A quick swing with her bat was all it took, and the girl fell to the ground. Melanie caught her before she could stain the cement with further injuries--she had no desire to clean any more messes today. She opened the front door and dragged the girl into the house, down into her room, and checked her pulse. She was still alive. Melanie reached into the bag the girl had brought with her--the one that contained such an important object. A boxcutter, bent and stained with a coppery smell, but still as sharp as it was yesterday evening when Melanie's mother left with it. What would the girl have even done, confronting her parents? She really ought to have gone to the police. It was good that Melanie's peers were so stupid, she supposed, even if it irked her.

Melanie listened to the sound of crashing upstairs. Her parents were awake, and she could smell popcorn popping from the kitchen. An unconventional breakfast, but one nonetheless. A simple knot would have to do for now. The girl would be dead by Saturday, anyway.

Plan B

A snippet from the *Clonage* Universe

She was slammed forward against the vehicle. The face shield on her helmet smacked hard against the door. The front end of the van had bits of metal poking out of it and SHEILA's interior systems began yelling sirens at her. With an anguished groan Alice managed to wrangle herself out of the shotgun seat belt and climb into the driver's seat. The holographic chaperone flickered in and out of view, finally collapsing as SHEILA started up the manual driving dashboard. The blue taxicab that had slammed directly into them sped off, leaving ominous black fumes in its wake.

"Oh, I don't feel so good..." Nans' voice came up from the backseat.

"How bad is it?" Alice struggled to maneuver SHEILA back onto the road. If they hurried, they'd be gone by the time the blue taxicab came back to make sure the deed was done.

"I think a panel in the back of my neck is poking through my skin... It hit the headrest really hard..." Nans sounded apologetic—or maybe her voice chip had been damaged. Alice would have to check that once they got to a safe place.

"Is Chesh okay?" The boy was mute, and Alice couldn't watch him sign while driving.

"Yeah, he's okay," Nans affirmed. "But I'm getting some blood on his clothes..."

Alice winced. "How badly are you bleeding?"

"I don't know... I can't tell if I'm technically still bleeding or not..."

"Ask Chesh and tell me what he thinks." A few beats of silence.

"He thinks I need a hospital."

Alice cursed and asked SHEILA to direct them to the nearest medical school. Hospitals would be a tad too interested in where their parents were. Undergrads could be bargained with.

"Chesh, you doing okay?" Alice sat next to him. It had started to rain, and so they had moved to a bench partially covered by the facade of the dorm wherein Nans was getting impromptu cyborg surgery.

Fine, you? He asked.

I'm worried. We can't hide forever. And I miss Mom. Alice signed.

We'll see her soon. Chesh smiled, his cheeks puffing out in that cute way of his.

"I'll get you guys somewhere safe, and then go back and explain everything." Alice held out a hand in the rain. "I'm sure she'll be excited to meet you, especially since you guys lived in her basement for so long without her knowledge."

Chesh laughed, his shoulders shaking and the sound of quiet wheezes cutting through the tension.

I always wanted a mom. Chesh admitted. *Nans is like my mom. She taught me to read.*

"And yet, you still can't tie your shoelaces. Most people, at age fourteen, can do at least that."

Most people didn't spend their childhood in a laboratory.

Alice nodded. Cars whirred past on the nearby road, much too fast for the speed limit, but hardly anyone cared. Some were green, or brown, or black, or gray—or red, but no blue. It should have been comforting.

SHEILA was easy to repair once Nans was all fixed up. Chesh slept on the roof of the dormitory and the helpful med student's engineering dormmate gave Alice the key to their workshop. By sunrise, the trio were long gone, and the two students were about two hundred dollars richer.

"Where are we going?" Nans fiddled with the knobs on the radio from the front seat.

"Wisconsin." Alice replied, relieved at no longer having to drive.

The cheese state?

"Yeah, the cheese state. Remember the woman who was at the bunker when I brought you two home?"

"Uh... no?" Nans picked a station and turned the volume up. "I was a little too unconscious at the time."

"Well, she's the reason the whole secret-underground-bunker-basement of mine exists." Alice's voice was kept intentionally light.

"So, she's the reason we're alive?" Nans looked out the window at the passing trees.

"Pretty much."

What's her name? Chesh signed.

Alice's smile turned sour and she grit her teeth. A complex emotion she couldn't begin to describe began to swirl in her gut.

"Let's just call her B."

Learning to Fall

A snippet from the *Local: Birth of a Vigilante* Universe

"Listen," Michael started, "if my future self doesn't appear to stop me, how bad of an idea can it really be?"

The moonlight had started to peak over the top of the skyline, and a cool wind threatened to throw Michael's twig-like body over the side of the roof. Soraya had to consciously restrain herself from dragging him away and calling this whole thing off. He'd insisted earlier today that she should teach him how to navigate the city--only his definition of 'navigate' clearly wasn't the same as her own.

"Just because I can jump that far doesn't mean you can! I've been training for years. You can't use me as a base for normalcy."

He rolled his eyes and muttered a, 'no kidding' under his breath. "Come on, just show me. I'll never learn if nobody teaches me!"

Soraya was self-taught, but she chose to keep that information to herself for now. Instead she straightened her back and evened her breathing before taking a running start. A well-timed ankle twist sent her arcing through the air, forty feet above the tiny little side street Michael had chosen. It was a little fascinating, though Michael would never admit it, to watch Soraya at work. It was even harder to admit that he was jealous as hell about it.

It took a half-second for Michael to realize she hadn't made it to the other side, plummeting out of view before she could make a grab for a handhold.

"So--Soraya?!" Michael could feel his whole body tense. Oh, crap! He got down on his hands and knees to peer over the side. His balance on the edge felt far more precarious now.

He couldn't see anything in the dim little alley, even with the neon signs on nearby buildings. No one replied. Michael felt his stomach lurch at the thought of what he might find at the bottom.

He stood and went a few paces away, trying to mimic her earlier pose: straightened back, evened breathing. He prepped himself to run--and then sprinted down the stairs, two at a time, cursing himself for suggesting this in the first place.

"Soraya? Where..." He stepped out into the side street, turning his phone on as a flashlight. A figure hung from the fire escape on the opposite building, held up by only a rope, limp and unmoving like a suicide.

"Oh *no*, Soraya--"

"BOO!" The body relinquished its hold on the rope, full-body tackling him into the ground.

"Soraya, oh my god, what the hell!" Michael clambered away from her, horrified at being tricked.

"You wanted me to teach you, right? Well the first thing you've got to learn is how to catch yourself when things go wrong," she got to her feet, her tone returning to its familiar strictness. "I'm just showing you the worst that could happen if something goes wrong."

"Jesus, well now I'm traumatized." Michael huffed.

"Better that than dead," Soraya reminded him, removing her makeshift rope--Michael recognized the belt, she'd been wearing it earlier--from the fire escape.

"Yeah. Better than dead," he agreed.

About the Author

Alexandra Babin is a junior student at Annapolis High School in the Performing and Visual Arts creative writing magnet program. *What Time of Year is it?* is her third publication, following *Ghost* and *Tell No One*. She recently met her newborn cousin, John Nester, for the first time. He was born at **7:32**am on February **9**th, **2019**, weighing **7**lbs. and **7.7**oz. John's older sister, Danielle, and his mother Karen have all been incredibly supportive throughout Alexandra's creative pursuits.

About the Illustrator

Katherine White is a junior student at Broadneck High School. She has worked with Alexandra Babin on a total of three pieces, including *Ghost* and *Tell No One*. Katherine is an aspiring agricultural scientist and has been drawing as a hobby since she was young.

www.ingramcontent.com/pod-product-compliance
Lightning Source LLC
Chambersburg PA
CBHW042324150426
43192CB00001B/35